☑ Y0-AAL-394

11 WAYS
— TO ENCOURAGE —
WORN OUT
VOLUNTEERS

BRANNON MARSHALL

© 2014 Awana® Clubs International

TABLE OF CONTENTS

MINISTRY CAN BE EXHAUSTING.

An essential part of being an effective ministry leader is encouraging those who serve with you.

As a leader, you hate to see volunteers step back because of burnout. You do everything in your power to prevent it. But burnout happens to great volunteers every year. It can be tough to encourage a volunteer who is feeling worn out. Sometimes you just don't know what to say. Sometimes your encouragement comes too late or in the wrong way.

Some the ideas in this book are preventative: practices and postures that help you anticipate volunteer discouragement before it ever shows up. Others are corrective: helping you lead volunteers who are already worn out, or discouraged through a healing process. Healthy leaders are attentive to both preventing and correcting volunteer burnout.

Whether you're reading this as a pastor, KidMin leader, or ministry leader, here are 11 ways to encourage worn out volunteers.

1

LEARN
TO LEAD THROUGH
EMPATHY

LEAD THROUGH EMPATHY

A friend loves at all times, and a brother is born for adversity. (Proverbs 17:17)

Empathy is the ability to feel hurt, take another's perspective, and connect with them. An empathetic connection brings healing, trust, and deeper relationships with those around you.

Express Resonance.
When a burned out volunteer opens up to you, he's taking a calculated risk. He's risking the chance that you won't understand — that you've never felt what he's feeling. If he's feeling loss, confusion, or anger, get to a place where you felt a similar emotion and reassure him that you get it.

Be Present.
In our constant-access world, the gift of your presence is rare. Empathy makes an exchange: Empathy takes the combined weight of everything you could be doing and gives it all up for the one thing you need to do.

- Keep your cell phone off the table.
- Turn the ringer off.
- Refuse to be interrupted.

Reflect.
Reflecting says to a tired volunteer: "What you're feeling is OK." Reflection can let her know that she's not crazy. She's not imagining things or emotionally off-base. Reflection isn't concerned with solving a problem as much as it is giving voice to feelings:

"I just don't know what to say."
"Man, that's tough."
"I'm so sorry you have to deal with that."

Leading with empathy takes work. But it can make all the difference for a worn-out volunteer.

2

SEND HANDWRITTEN

NO

Your

avoid the
too today!

YOU'VE
GOT
TH IS
JENNY!

TES

OF ENCOURAGEMENT

Realm life!

SEND HANDWRITTEN
NOTES OF ENCOURAGEMENT

Everyone wants to feel like they're appreciated, like they matter, like they're a part of something important.

Most volunteers in your church serve because they genuinely love children and youth. They aren't looking for recognition. They aren't chasing trophies. But — although they'll never ask for it — most would love a nod of appreciation from you.

In the fast-paced era of email, texting, and digital communication, writing a note by hand means a lot. Why? Because writing notes by hand takes time. It takes thought. It means that people are worth more to you than just a quick email.

You might even get creative by investing in some personal stationary or letterhead. Consider keeping a record of notes that you've sent so that no one gets overlooked. Include personal comments about how you're seeing God working in a volunteer's life, ministry, or family.

Expressing appreciation is more than just a strategy for retention. Showing gratitude, love, thankfulness, and respect are part of what it means to be a faithful extension of Body of Christ.

3

PRACTICE REMARKABLE PEOPLE SKILLS

REMARKABLE PEOPLE SKILLS

Healthy volunteers are led by remarkable leaders. Remarkable leaders constantly develop skills that nourish their teams:

Anticipation
Sense peoples' needs before they even have to say anything. Think of the long time waitress at the town diner: When regular customers walk in, she might ask: "Having the usual today?" Anticipation means knowing your team and honoring their preferences.

Generosity
Generosity includes giving your time, energy, and resources. Invite others to go with them in their journey. Be selfless. Freely give to others and pass on what you've learned.

Troubleshooting

When something goes wrong, don't be content to merely provide people with instructions for the solution. Work with your team – in most cases for them – to make sure the trouble is resolved. Troubleshooting means that you'll be involved. You'll be a solution provider.

Individuality

Understand that the volunteers who serve in your church aren't just cogs in a machine. They are individuals. God has given every volunteer a unique gifting, personality, a suite of strengths according to His plan. Provide volunteers a sense of stability by affirming their individual gifts.

4

ASK QUESTIONS

THAT SPARK
CONVERSATION

ASK QUESTIONS THAT SPARK
GENUINE CONVERSATION

Good people can become exhausted when they feel like no one is interested in them.
Without a sense of community, even the most faithful volunteers can wither and fade. Build compassion and community with your volunteers by learning to ask good questions.

Good questions express genuine interest and spark genuine conversation. Questions like:

• How can I help you?
• Can I get you anything?
• How can I pray for you?
• Can I share what you're up to with others?
• How is your family?
• If I could alleviate one tension, what would it be?
• How can I do better?
• Is there anything else that you'd rather do?

Schedule one-on-ones with volunteers.
Be sensitive to times that are convenient for them.

Assure volunteers that their transparency is valuable to you.

Good questions communicate that you're in the trenches with your volunteers. While taking the time to foster this kind of conversation feels exhausting in the moment, it's your ability to take their perspective, withhold your judgment, and feel with them that makes you a remarkable leader.

A word of warning: Be prepared. You might get more than you bargained for. You might trigger a frustrated volunteer. You might stumble upon someone who's approaching burnout. Show your commitment by giving them your full attention, expressing your support, and following through on their needs.

5

GIVE
THEM A BREAK

OCTOBER 8

TAKE THE DAY OFF

GIVE THEM A BREAK

Part of the sting of burnout is the guilt associated with admitting that it's real.
Faithful volunteers usually don't like to admit that they might need to take a break. Strong leaders provide stability by letting volunteers know a season of rest is OK. Start by building intentionality into your relationships.

• Check in with volunteers on a regular basis.
• Be sensitive to early signs of fatigue.
• Actively seek out conversation.
• Encourage them to take a break.

Some volunteers are content to serve in one ministry for years. Others appreciate the freedom to serve in different areas from year to year. A period of rest can yield great insights for volunteers who may have been stuck in a ministry rut or need a recharge.

Giving exhausted leaders a break will likely result in a shift of ministry focus or interest. They might discover that God is asking them to engage in ministry opportunities they hadn't previously considered. Be encouraged by that. While you might lose a volunteer in the short-term, you have the opportunity to build the church in the long-term.

6 REFRAME

COMM

REFRAME COMMITMENT

Volunteers don't commit to a ministry because they want to do you a favor. They commit because they believe in what serving represents: leading kids and helping them follow Jesus.

But often, our appeal for volunteers sounds like begging.

We casually say things like:
- "We need someone to staff the kids counter this Wednesday night."
- "We're low on volunteers for VBS. Can anyone help out?"
- "We're looking for people to help out with."

While these appeals aren't necessarily wrong, they mistakenly communicate that ministry commitment is primarily a task that needs to be done. When ministry becomes a task, it's easy to let it wear you out.

Consider how you can turn that expectation upside down. Consider phrasing your appeal for volunteers in terms of what they get out of it:

• An opportunity to serve as part of a great team
• An opportunity to spread hope, joy, and love
• An opportunity to share Jesus with kids
• An opportunity to shape the church

The key with reframing commitment is to deliver on what you promise. Build personal and spiritual growth into your volunteer opportunities. Equip volunteers with only the best tools. Make any training as excellent as possible. Make volunteering at your church incredible.

GET
PERSONAL

7

GET PERSONAL

Everyone wants to be known.
But often, ministry volunteers are known for their
gifts, where they serve, or how long they've served.
Those facts are important, but they're not enough.
Getting personal with your volunteers means that
you know them, lead them, and affirm them for
more than just their performance.

- Remember significant events like birthdays,
  anniversaries, etc.
- Get to know what makes them feel loved and
  appreciated.
- Get to know their family: spouses, children,
  and parents.
- Plan your ministry calendar with their family
  in mind.
- Ask how you can pray for them. And do it.
- Learn about their hobbies and interests.
- Ask about what's important to them.

Getting personal also means that volunteers know each other. Maintaining a strong sense of community is a crucial factor in volunteer retention as well as personal development.

You might host focused, team-building events prior to meeting time where volunteers can talk through ministry needs, share their stories, pray together, and get to know each other.

Elevating personal relationships as a ministry priority will cost you. You'll carry peoples' burdens *with* them. You'll often extend yourself beyond your comfort zone. But the risk will always pay off over time.

8

SHEPHERD BY SERVING

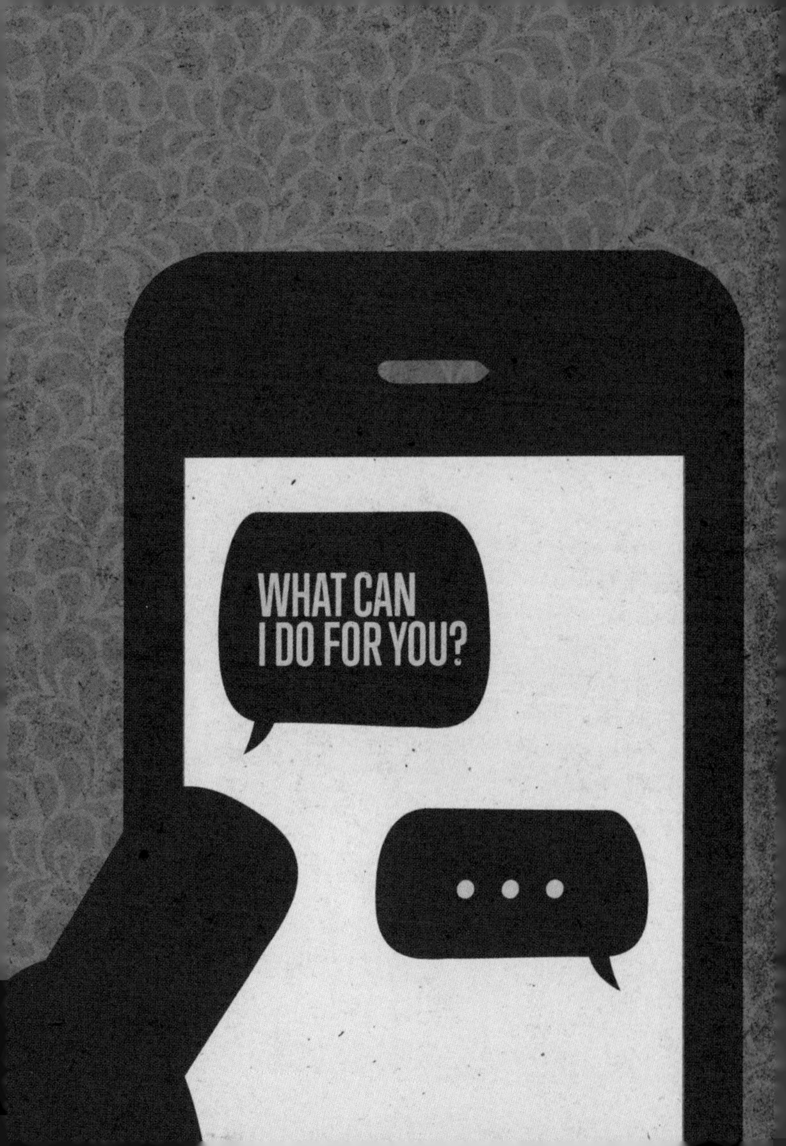
WHAT CAN
I DO FOR YOU?

SHEPHERD BY SERVING

He who is least among you all is the one who is great. (Luke 9:48b)

Leadership is not about what you can do, what you can change, or what you can offer.

These ideas may be partly true, but leaders are first and foremost servants. Taking the posture of a servant is a powerful way to create a healthy team culture.

Serving volunteers means putting their needs before your own. It means continually asking questions like: What do *they* need? What's on *their* mind? What can I do for *them*? Over time, asking thoughtful questions will develop into posture of servanthood and will result in an encouragement for your worn-out leaders.

- Deflect praise and absorb blame.
- Give affirmation whenever possible.
- Let volunteers contribute to vision and direction.
- Tell volunteers that you're thankful for them. And why.
- Look for opportunities to celebrate their accomplishments.

Leaders who see themselves as servants attract and retain great volunteers.

9
COMMUNICATE
WELL

COMMUNICATE WELL

Few things can frustrate volunteers more quickly than poor communication.
Creating a ministry culture of great communication will have the double effect of preventing volunteer fatigue while providing a space for healing.

Their Style › Your Style
Everyone has a communication style that is most natural to them. Honor your volunteers by using their communication style. You might have to work at this, but adjusting your communication style is a great way to show them that you care.

Listening › Talking
Your leaders probably know you better than you know them. They hear from you often and have learned your leadership style. But a worn out leader needs a listener first. Listening may take the form of quick discussion, or building regular feedback opportunities for volunteers.

Understanding › Problem Solving

Whatever help you can provide to a discouraged volunteer isn't as important as what you understand about them. However you create a listening platform, make it your primary goal to understand where they're coming from. What are they feeling? What are they frustrated about? Why do they feel that way?

Follow up › Quick Fix

Discouraged volunteers will appreciate that you've taken the time to understand them. But that appreciation can quickly fade unless you support them. Circle back with volunteers who are going through a tough season. Ask how they're doing. Express your desire to be a support. Be specific.

10

GIVE
GIVE

GENEROUSLY   PRACTICALLY

GIVE PRACTICALLY
GIVE GENEROUSLY

Many seek the favor of a generous man.
(Proverbs 19:6a)

Discouragement and burnout are hard to measure. Discouragement affects our hearts, our motivation, our self-esteem, and our ability to grow. But unseen pains can sometimes be eased by visible acts of generosity.

Get them a gift.
A gift is a small way of saying "thanks" while also speaking to the interests of the individual.
A great book. A cup of coffee. A conversation or a meal that you pay for. The most meaningful gifts usually aren't expensive. But they are always thoughtful.

Bless their family.
Consider what the volunteers in your ministry
sacrifice in order to serve. Their family also gives.
Over time, that pace can get tiring. A gift card for
a family dinner can make a huge difference for a
family who also carries the emotional burden of
ministry.

Give Generously.
If you're able, allocate ministry resources in your
budget for generous giving. Make generosity a
priority — not a last minute thought.

Building a culture of generosity can be a blast.
Making sure people feel valued raises the bar of
expectation for potential future volunteers.

11

TAKE CARE OF YOURSELF

TAKE CARE OF YOURSELF

Accepting your limits is part what it means to be
an effective leader over the long-term. But many
leaders live too close to their limits with disastrous
consequences.

Living too close to your limits hurts those who serve with
you. They don't receive the care that they need and you
feel like you're constantly pulled in 1000 directions.

Regularly ask yourself the following questions:
- Do you wish you could be honest about stress you feel?
- Do you entertain the notion of quitting, but talk yourself
  out of it?
- Do you wish you could open up to someone, but can't?
- Do you frequently feel tried or worn out?
- Do you dread upcoming conversations?
- Do you often feel alone?

If you find yourself in any of those places regularly, it's
time to ask for help. If you're totally on your own, it might
even be time to suspend ministry activity for a season.

Your spiritual health and the health of those around you are more important than maintaining ministry inertia.

How many volunteers can I effectively serve? That's a question that only you can answer. Remember: Healthy ministry isn't about more. It's about better. By being attentive to your team's needs and your ability to care for them thoughtfully and selflessly, your ministry will be known as a healthy and enjoyable place to serve.

BRANNON MARSHALL

With a background in church planting and pastoral ministry, Brannon's passion centers on pastoral leadership, missiology, and church health. Brannon serves as the Director of Global Church Engagement with Awana where he leads strategy on equipping churches for ministry success.

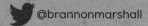 @brannonmarshall  awana.org/blog